FUN FAX

Written by Jill Price
Illustrated by Barry Green

Henderson Publishing
Woodbridge, England

1 LUMBER JACK

Jack saws a tree trunk in half, then half again; then he halved all the pieces once more.
If the trunk was originally 8 metres long, how long is each piece now?

2 NUMBER CROSSWORD

ACROSS

1. 31 + 16
3. 127 × 5
6. 322 + 167
8. 47 + 14
9. 96 × 6
12. 633 – 224
14. 163 + 759
16. 12 × 7
18. 94 – 37
19. 82 × 5

DOWN

1. 11 × 4
2. 157 × 5
4. 6 × 6
5. 74 × 7
7. 10,000 – 258
10. 12 × 5
11. 15 × 13
13. 555 + 426
15. 9 × 3
17. 101 – 61

3 NICE DICE

Opposite sides of a dice always add up to 7. (But you knew that already, didn't you!) Can you fill in the missing numbers on these shapes which, incidentally, can all be made into dice.

4 SHEEP TRIP

By the time Farmer Harris had made five journeys, his trailer had carried a total of 500 sheep. There were 190 sheep altogether on the first two trips; 155 sheep altogether on the second and third trips; 210 sheep altogether on the third and fourth trips; and 225 sheep altogether on the fourth and fifth trips.

How many sheep were on the trailer on the third trip?

5 HIDDEN MONEY

Bank Robber, Nasher Noggins, has hidden the loot somewhere in the park. By doing these easy sums, you can discover the hiding place! Begin with the square marked START, moving on to the square with the same number as the answer of the last sum. (Your clue is the letter written beside the number.) Carry on to the sum immediately below, and so on. Good hunting!

START 3 + 7	12: B 10 x 4	32: V 11 x 3	67: O 93 – 47	42: X 19 + 18	46: T 78 – 19	90: I 48 + 57	36: R 3 x 7
80: M 48 – 25	26: G 8 x 4	21: I 47 + 7	17: E 1 x 47	35: T 97 – 46	11: P 18 + 4	31: B 32 + 35	27: G 9 x 9
6: – 31 + 19	33: W 49 – 8	50: A 8 x 7	92: S 10 x 10	10: B 19 – 3	18: O 18 – 5	59: T 59:14	54: E 9 – 7
29: I 14 – 7	89: O 2 x 35	41: H 6 x 7	99: – 18 + 11	40: A 14 + 13	24: Q 6 x 3	56: – 4 x 3	70: F 7 x 13
105: T END	15: D 5 x 5	60: E 19 x 4	81: – 6 x 5	49: N 41 + 21	22: H 4 + 13	48: T 11 x 2	2: D 33 x 3
25: Y 46 – 20	16: U 4 x 9	13: R 5 x 3	51: H 20 x 3	91: – 7 x 5	88: P 10 x 9	8: – 51 – 3	23: – 54 + 35
100: A 63 – 14	63: T 4 x 2	76: – 23 x 4	47: – 15 + 16	7: N 24 ÷ 4	30: A 9 x 7	73: O 4 x 20	62: D 11 x 8

6 WEIGH IT UP

Study these pictures and calculate which side of the scales will weigh more in the last picture.

7 SPOTTY SUMS

If you've got some dominoes, try laying them out to make sums . . . like this:

	3	4		1
				3
1	0		2	3

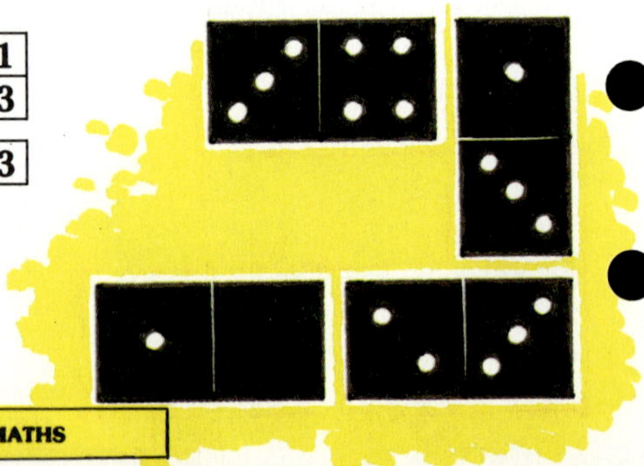

8 ODD NUMBERS

Try adding four odd numbers to make a total of 10. How many different ways can you do it?

9 ICE CREAM

Nasher can eat an ice cream in 3 minutes. How many can he eat in half an hour?

10 BOXES

A game for 2 players
You'll need a pencil each

* Spin a coin to see who goes first
* The first player joins one dot to another (across or down but *not* diagonally)
* The second player does the same
* When the fourth side of the box is filled in, that player writes his initial inside the box and goes again
* The idea is to see who can complete the most boxes

Like this:

You can easily make your own dotty grids — as huge as you like!

1st player			**2nd player**		
Game One	☐	boxes	Game One	☐	boxes
Game Two	☐	boxes	Game Two	☐	boxes
Game Three	☐	boxes	Game Three	☐	boxes
Game Four	☐	boxes	Game Four	☐	boxes

11 THREE-SIDED MAGIC

Can you add the numbers 3, 4, 5, 6, 7 and 8 along the sides of this triangle so that each side adds up to 13?

12 QUICKIE

You have the same amount of money in your pocket as your mate. How much should you give him so that he has got 10p more than you?

13 POTTY PROBLEM

Here is an arrangement of flower pots. Can you number each pot from 1 to 14 so that each row of four adds up to 30? Some numbers have been put in to start you off.

14 NINES

Here's an unusual way to learn your nine times table. For example, to work out 4 × 9, look at number four on the outside of the ring, then read across the wiggly line to the numbers inside the ring. Answer 36.

Now try these:

2 × 9 =
3 × 9 =
5 × 9 =
6 × 9 =
7 × 9 =
8 × 9 =

15 HIDDEN NUMBERS

In all the following sums the answer is hidden in the numbers on the right. Can you circle each answer?

1.	19 × 23	=	2 4 3 7
2.	580 ÷ 20	=	2 9 0
3.	847 − 593	=	1 2 5 4
4.	3 × 98	=	2 9 4 0
5.	189 ÷ 9	=	1 2 1
6.	68 + 57	=	1 1 2 5
7.	19 × 12	=	1 2 2 8
8.	309 − 88	=	2 2 1 2

16 CHOCOLATE SQUARES

Here is a slab of chocolate squares. Nasher and Neescha want exactly the same amount. How would you divide the chocolate with one straight cut, starting from the arrow?

17 STAR QUEST

Can you add the missing numbers, from 1 to 12, to make the sum of each line the same?

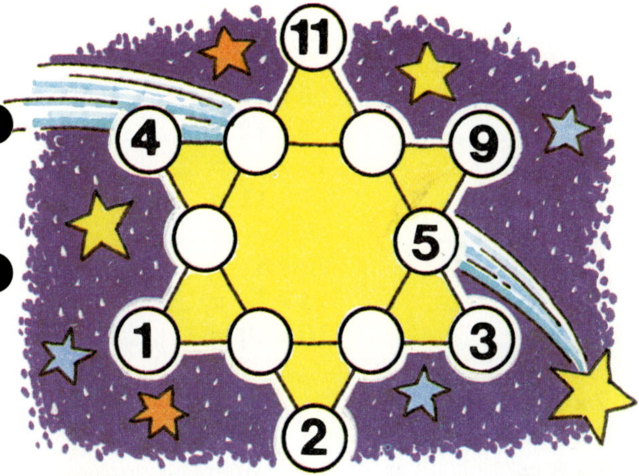

18 CARRY ON CAMPING

At the campsite, campers are sheltering from the rain. They huddle inside two tents. If one camper runs from one tent to the other, the number of campers inside the second tent would be three times the number inside the first tent.

If one camper ran from the second tent to the first, the number of campers in both tents would be equal.

How many campers are there in each of the tents?

19 DOTTY PROBLEM

Work out the answers to the sums. Then, in numerical order, join up the dots to reveal the picture.

$2 \times 3 =$ ______
$3 \times 3 =$ ______
$5 \times 3 =$ ______
$3 \times 9 =$ ______
$19 \times 2 =$ ______
$6 \times 7 =$ ______
$11 \times 4 =$ ______
$9 \times 5 =$ ______
$10 \times 5 =$ ______
$9 \times 6 =$ ______
$7 \times 9 =$ ______
$8 \times 8 =$ ______
$9 \times 8 =$ ______

$3 \times 26 =$ ______
$10 \times 8 =$ ______
$7 \times 12 =$ ______
$29 \times 3 =$ ______
$8 \times 11 =$ ______
$19 \times 5 =$ ______
$12 \times 8 =$ ______
$14 \times 7 =$ ______
$10 \times 10 =$ ______

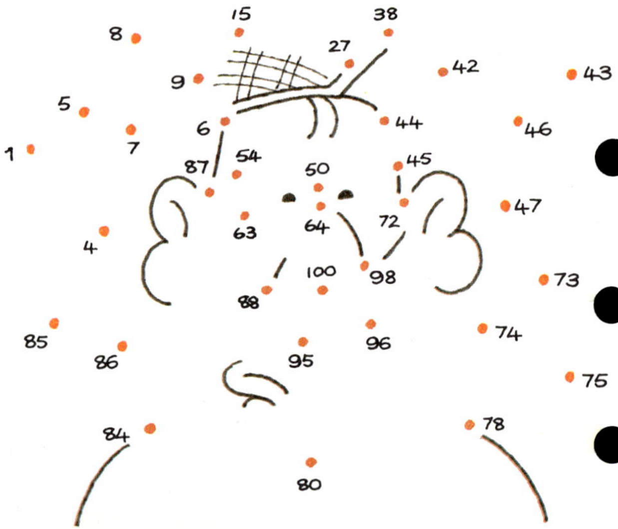

20 BAGS OF COMICS

Tricky Tim carried home nine comics and four carrier bags. Somehow he'd managed to put an odd number of comics into each bag without cutting either the comics or the bags. How?

21 PICTURE QUIZ

Solve each picture puzzle and then change the number to a letter.
A = 1, B = 2, C = 3, etc.

36 apples altogether.
How many in each bag?

Weight needed to balance the scales

How many hours before midnight?

How many sugar lumps are left if the horse eats half?

How many can you eat?

Count the number of cubes.

Clue: An exciting book!

22 FARMER'S FIELD

Can you divide Farmer Harris' field into six separate sections so that each section contains a tree, a cow, a tractor and a milkchurn?

23 CODE BREAKERS

A	B	C	D	E	F	G	H	I	J	K	L	M	N	O	P	Q	R	S	T	U	V	W	X	Y	Z
1	2	3	3	5	6	7	8	9	10	11	12	13	14	15	16	17	18	19	20	21	22	23	24	25	26

Can you decode this sentence? All you have to do is add, multiply or subtract the numbers and fill in the appropriate letter that the answer stands for.

3×3, $3 \times 2 / 5^2$, $10 + 5$, $7 \times 3 / 4 - 1$, 1^2, $4^2 - 2 / 20 - 4 + 3$, 5×3, 4×3, 11×2, $4 + 1 / 10 \times 2$, $4 + 4$, 3^2, $4^2 + 3 / 0 + 3$, $4^2 - 1$, $2 + 2$, $6 - 1 / 16 + 7$, $5 + 3$, $12 + 13 / 7 \times 2$, $9 + 6$, $4 \times 5 / 8 + 5$, $9 - 8$, $3^2 + 2$, $2^2 + 1 / 7 \times 3$, $4^2 / 5^2$, $8 + 7$, $19 + 2$, $6 \times 3 / 4^2 - 1$, $15 + 8$, $7 + 7$?

Now try this one:

4×3, $3 + 2$, $21 - 20$, $9 + 9$, 7×2, 3^2, 2×7, $6 + 1 / 6 + 7$, $0 + 1$, 4×5, $3^2 - 1$, $11 + 8 / 10 \times 2$, 4×2, 3^2, $7 + 12 / 15 + 8$, $0^2 + 1$, $5 \times 5 / 1^2 + 2$, $4 - 3$, $9 + 5 / 1 + 1$, $16 - 11 / 24 - 18$, 7×3, $36 - 22$!

24 SUM TOTAL

Cross out 11 of these numbers so that the remaining 10 numbers add up to 62.

6 6 6 6 6 6 6
8 8 8 8 8 8 8
4 4 4 4 4 4 4

25 DOT SPOT

No, this isn't another game of Boxes (see Puzzle 10)!
Can you draw four straight lines through eight dots to make a square which will leave seventeen holes inside and twenty-four holes outside that square?

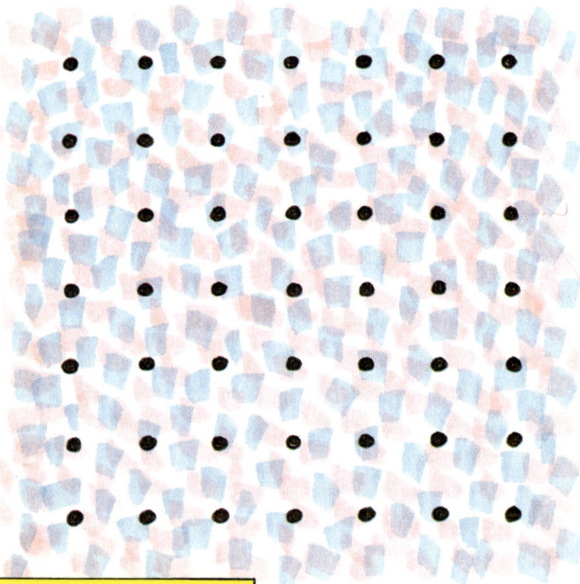

26 LOG PROB

Jack has three piles of logs with eleven logs in one pile, seven in the next and six in the last.
He wants three equal piles, i.e. eight logs in each.
Easy enough, yes! But there is a strict rule – you may only add to one pile the same number that are already in that pile. In other words, you can only put six logs on the pile that has six logs.
Try to do it in three moves.

27 CARRY COP!

P.C. Smith lifted P.C. Clark and P.C. Baker held P.C. Clark's legs. Then P.C. Baker lifted P.C. Clark with P.C. Smith holding P.C. Clark's legs. If each policeman has a go at being lifted, in how many ways can they lift each other?

28 QUICKIE

If you put three plus (+) signs and one minus (–) sign between the numbers on the page, the sum will be correct.

9 8 7 6 5 4 3 2 1 = 100

29 BOTTLE IT!

One bottle contains water and the other orange juice. If Wendy pours a little bit of water into the juice bottle, and the same amount back into the water bottle, will there be more water in the orange than there is orange in the water?

30 NOUGHTS AND CROSSES – WITH A DIFFERENCE!

Use the digits 0 to 9 . . . and use them only once in a game. The winner is the first person to make a line of three digits which add up to 10.

e.g.

2		5
	1	
4		

31 ROUNDABOUT SUMS

Naughty Nasher is trapped by the police — or is he? Do the sums at each roundabout, beginning top left, and follow the route of the correct answer. If you get your sums right, Nasher might make a run for it to the right exit!

A
B
11
C
36
40
4×5
10
4×12
21
16
19
47
48
D
27
9
16
2×7
E
15
13
14
55
15
10×5
500
101
10×11
46
21
110
8×6
48
38
F
12
3×3
9
6

32 THE FARMER AND HIS PEN

Now that he's got all his sheep back on the farm (see Puzzle 4), Farmer Harris has to put them into the sheep pens in the yard. He used to have thirteen fences which made four pens, like this

But he's just found an extra one and can now make seven separate pens.
How does he do it?

33 WATCH OUT NASHER!

Nasher Noggins has been given two watches for his birthday! The only trouble is neither of them works properly — one loses an hour every day and the other has stopped completely. Which watch do you think is the more accurate?

34 SPORTS STARS

Wendy and Nigel and their friends Tracy and Kevin are sitting round a table in the classroom. All four have just won first prize in throwing, sprinting, hurdles and high jump.

Study these clues and then work out who is the sprint champ:

1. The best thrower is sitting on Wendy's left.

2. The highest jumper is directly opposite Nigel.

3. Tracy and Kevin are next to each other.

4. There is a girl to the left of the hurdler.

35 THAT'S ODD!

Add up these sums and you might find a surprising answer . . .

222	132	131	332
111	213	223	121
+ 333	+ 321	+ 312	+ 213

36 QUICKIE

This peacock's feathers measure 1 metre when they are stretched out. How many peacocks can you put in an empty cage which measures 4.5 metres by 3 metres by 4.5 metres?

37 MUSEUM TRIP

Wendy and Nigel are on their school trip to a museum — and they are dead bored! To make it more fun they have decided to visit each section of the museum once only. How did they manage to see each part without going back through the same section twice? Work out the route in letter sequence.

38 PARK PROBLEM

On his way to the park, Nasher counts 43 fence posts, each one exactly 1 metre apart. How long is the fence?

39 NUMBER CRUNCHER

Fill in the missing numbers:

a. 0 2 __ 6 8 10
b. 1 4 9 16 25 __
c. 1 __ 5 7 9 11 13
d. 1 1 2 3 5 __ 13
e. 0 2 5 9 __ 20
f. 1 3 9 __ 81 243
g. 2 3 5 9 17 __ 65
h. 1 4 6 9 11 __

40 SQUARE DEAL

How many squares are there?

41 HOW OLD?

Matthew is 6 years older than Lucy.
Next year he will be twice as old as her.
How old is Matthew?
How old is Lucy?

42 SWEETS GALORE

Neescher says she'll sell Wendy
four chocolate bars and three packets of crisps for 37p
or
three chocolate bars and four packets of crisps for 33p
How much is a bar of chocolate?
How much is a packet of crisps?

43 ROLL-A-POSER

Our picture shows a huge wooden block set on three wheels. Each wheel has a circumference of 2 metres. The block is moved until each wheel has made a complete turn.
How far has the block travelled?

44 GREEDY GRUB

This hungry grub eats his own bodyweight every day. On day 12 he weighs 12 grammes.

On which day did the grub weigh 3 grammes?

45 STEEPLE JACK

Jack's job is to repair chimneys — the big ones in the town, not just the small ones on our houses. He has to reach the top of a very tall chimney to do some repair work. It's 120 metres high. In one hour, Jack climbs 40 metres up the giant face of the chimney. But he slips 30 metres downwards again! (Don't worry — Jack is tied on with a rope!)
How long will it take Jack to reach the top?

46 CROSS COUNTRY

There are nine countries on this map. How can a tourist travel through each country by crossing each border exactly once?

47 THE MISSING LINK?

Harry, the railway engineer, is faced with a problem. The extra-strong chain he uses to pull trucks behind the engine has broken — into five pieces! (The broken sections of chain are shown in our picture.)

It takes Harry half an hour to open up one link and join it to another.

What is the minimum time necessary for Harry to join up the five sections of chain again?

48 CAULIFLOWER CONUNDRUM

At the market two green-grocers were selling potatoes. One stall-keeper gave a free cauliflower to every customer who bought two bags of his new potatoes. The other stall-keeper gave away a cauliflower with each bag of potatoes sold.

When the market opened early in the morning, both stalls had an equal number of bags. They had an equal number of cauliflowers to sell, too. By the end of the day, one stall had no cauliflowers left but still had five bags of potatoes. The other stall had sold all its potatoes but had five cauliflowers left to sell.

If every customer at the first stall bought two bags of potatoes, how many bags and cauliflowers did each stall-keeper have to begin with?

49 PLIMSOLL-LINE POSER

An oil-tanker is moored in the dock. It has a measured scale painted down its side. At low tide, the water level reads 8″ on this scale. The water in the dock rises 5″ at high tide. How many inches of the painted scale will be below water at high tide?

50 JUGGLING WITH PLATES

Have you ever seen Jugglers on the stage who keep a long row of plates carefully balanced on thin rods — the trick is to run and twirl the plates just before they lose their spin and topple off onto the floor!
Here's a juggling trick you can do without running around the room! All you have to do is arrange the seven plates in six rows. Each row must be made of three plates. Sounds easy? We'll see . . . .

51 THE ALCHEMIST

Aristotle the Alchemist mixes his strange potions in four special jars. Any volume of liquid (or magic potion) in exact pints up to 15 pints could be measured using these four jars, without using any jar more than once. How much liquid does each jar hold?

52 THE ROUND TABLE

Four friends, Jim, Ted, Brian and Peter are a teacher, a mechanic, a shop-keeper and a fireman, although not in that order. They are sitting around a table having supper together, with Jim seated to the left of the teacher, and the mechanic to the right of Brian. The shop-keeper is facing Peter. Who is the fireman?

53 JOLLY HOCKEY STICKS

In a school tournament, three hockey teams, A, B and C, each had to play two matches against each of the other teams.
The total number of goals scored during the entire tournament was 11. Team A alone scored 4 goals. Team C did not score at all. Team A won all their matches and no two matches ended up with the same result. What was the result in each match?

54 MATHEMATICAL MARATHON

In a half-Marathon, the runner who was three places in front of the runner who finished sixth was five places ahead of the runner who finished last.
How many runners completed the race?

ANSWERS

1 Lumber Jack

One metre, unless you cut it lengthwise, in which case it would still be eight metres long!

2 Number Crossword

(1) 4	(2) 7	■	(3) 6	(4) 3	(5) 5
(6) 4	8	(7) 9	■	(8) 6	1
■	(9) 5	7	(10) 6	■	8
(11) 1	■	(12) 4	0	(13) 9	■
(14) 9	(15) 2	2	■	(16) 8	(17) 4
(18) 5	7	■	(19) 4	1	0

3 Nice Dice

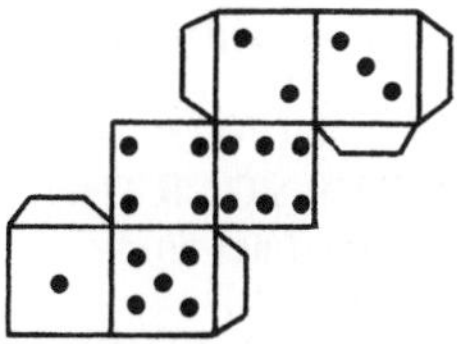

4 Sheep Trip

There were 190 sheep on the first two trips, and 225 sheep on the fourth and fifth trips, which makes a total of 415 sheep. So on the third trip there were 500 – 415 = 85 sheep.

5 Hidden Money

BURIED-IN-A-BAG-AT-THE-BOTTOM-OF-THE-SANDPIT

6 Weigh it up

The teapot and cups weigh more.

8 Odd Numbers

Here are three different ways:

1 + 1 + 3 + 5
1 + 1 + 1 + 7
1 + 3 + 3 + 3

9 Ice Cream

Nasher would be able to eat 10 ice creams . . . although he'd probably be sick!

11 Three-Sided Magic

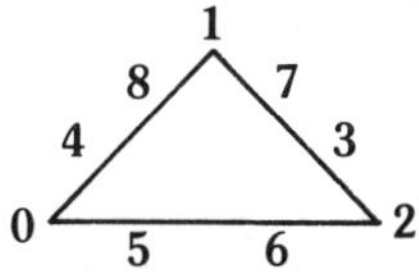

12 Quickie

You should give your mate 5p

13 Potty Problem

14 Nines

$2 \times 9 = 18$ $6 \times 9 = 54$
$3 \times 9 = 27$ $7 \times 9 = 63$
$5 \times 9 = 45$ $8 \times 9 = 72$

15 Hidden Numbers

1. 437
2. 29
3. 254
4. 294
5. 21
6. 125
7. 228
8. 221

16 Chocolate Squares
Cut the slab of chocolate like this:

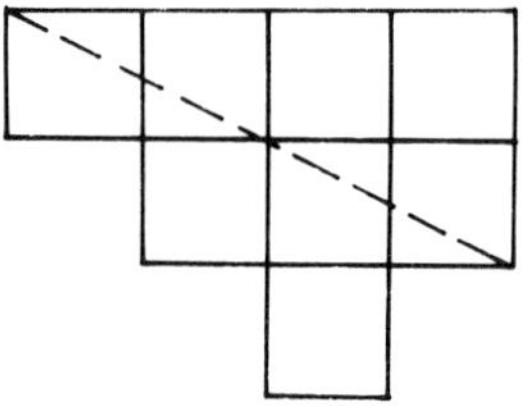

17 Star Quest

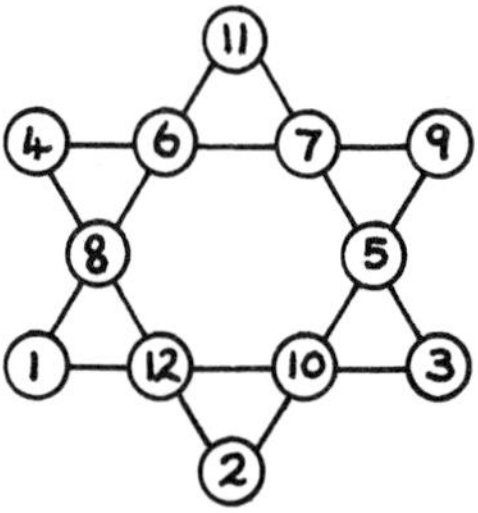

18 Carry On Camping
3 and 5.

19 Dotty Problem

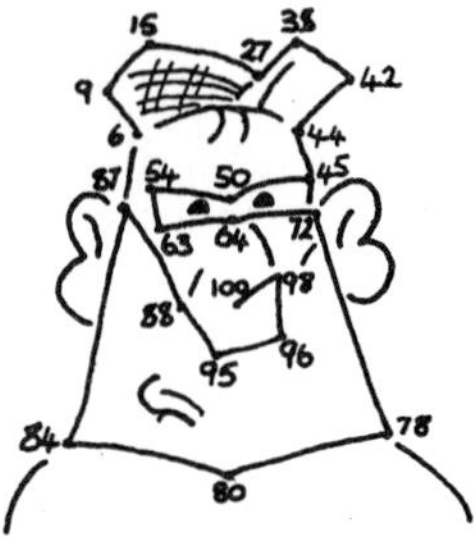

20 Bags of Comics
Tim put three comics into three bags and then put those three bags into the fourth bag!

21 Picture Quiz
F U N F A X

22 Farmers Field

23 Codebreakers
The first sentence reads:
IF YOU CAN SOLVE THIS CODE WHY NOT MAKE UP YOUR OWN?
The second sentence reads:
LEARNING MATHS THIS WAY CAN BE FUN!

24 Sum Total
Cross out 6 sixes, 2 eights and three fours.

25 Dot Spot

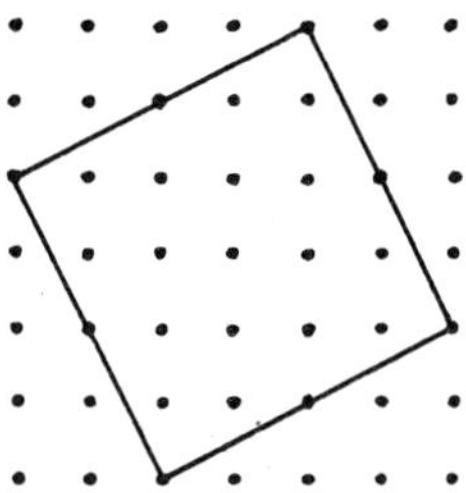

26 Log Prob
Start with 11 7 6
1st move: Take 7 from the pile of 11 logs and move them to the pile of 7 logs. i.e. 4 14 6
2nd move: Take six from that new pile of 14 and move them to the pile of 6 logs. i.e. 4 8 12
3rd move: Take 4 from the new pile of 12 and move them to the first pile. i.e. 8 8 8

27 Carry Cop!
The policemen can lift each other in six different ways.

29 Bottle It!
No, there is the same in each bottle.

31 Roundabout Sums
Nasher chooses Exit F.

32 The Farmer And His Pen

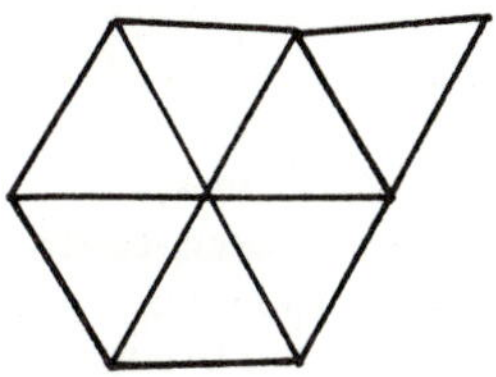

33 Watch Out Nasher!
The watch that has stopped completely is more accurate because it is right twice a day. The other one would only be right every twelve days.

34 Sports Stars
Wendy is the sprint champ. This is how they were sitting:

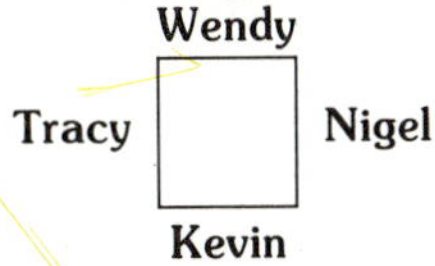

36 Quickie
One peacock — then the cage won't be empty any more! Ouch!

37 Museum Trip
The route is

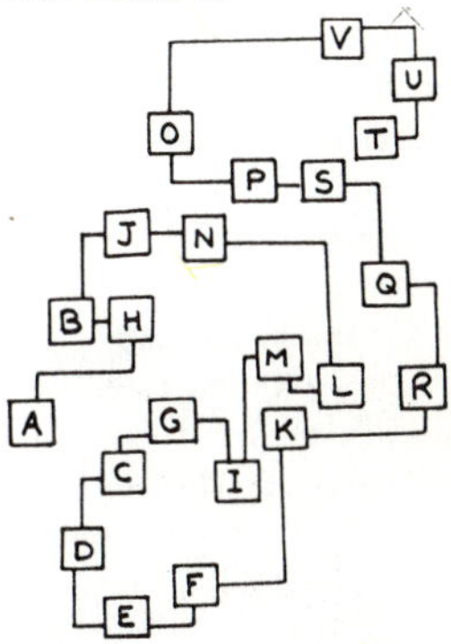

38 Park Problem
The fence is 42 metres long.

39 Number Cruncher

a. 4	e. 14
b. 36	f. 27
c. 3	g. 33
d. 8	h. 14

40 Square Deal
There are 14 squares

41 How Old?
Matthew is 11
Lucy is 5

42 Sweets Galore
A bar of chocolate costs 7p and crisps cost 3p.

43 Roll-a-Poser
You must think of two different movements here — the block over the wheels and the wheels on the ground. When the wheels have made a complete turn, the block has moved 2 metres over the wheels and the wheels have moved 2 metres on the ground so the block has travelled 4 metres.

44 Greedy Grub
On day 10.

45 Steeple Jack
12 hours.

46 Cross Country

47 The Missing Link
It will take Harry at least 1 hour 30 minutes. He only needs to open up the 3 link section to make 3 individual links. With these he can join the remaining 4 sections together.

48 Cauliflower Conundrum
Each stall had 20 bags of potatoes and 15 cauliflowers at the beginning.

49 Plimsoll-Line Poser
The same as at low tide — 8″. The rise in water level has no effect on this scale because a ship floats ON the water. The Plimsoll-line will only alter if the tanker is loaded or unloaded.

50 Juggling With Plates

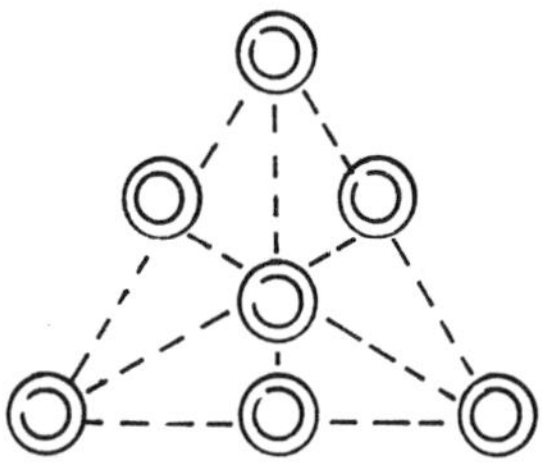

51 The Alchemist
1, 2 4 and 8 pints.

52 The Round Table
Ted is the fireman. He is sitting facing Brian.

53 Jolly Hockey Sticks
A v B 2 – 1, 1 – 1
A v C 1 – 0, 0 – 0
B v C 2 – 0, 3 – 0

54 Mathematical Marathon
Eight runners